# ANNO DOMINI

# Anno Domini

## Ed Block

*Foreword by Angela Alaimo O'Donnell*

WIPF & STOCK · Eugene, Oregon

ANNO DOMINI

Wipf & Stock
An Imprint of Wipf and Stock Publishers
199 W. 8th Ave., Suite 3
Eugene, OR 97401

www.wipfandstock.com

PAPERBACK ISBN: 978-1-5326-0170-5
HARDCOVER ISBN: 978-1-5326-0172-9

Manufactured in the U.S.A.                    SEPTEMBER 23, 2016

*To my wife and my family*

# TABLE OF CONTENTS

THE THIRTY-NINE POEMS IN this spare and elegant collection constitute a pilgrim's almanac. Ed Block's *Anno Domini* charts the seasons of the liturgical year, beginning with the anti-climax of post-Christmas Ordinary Time, following the speaker through Lenten observance, Easter dawn, recollection of moments in the life of Christ, and closing the circle with the return of Advent and the celebration of Christ's coming. This is the Alpha and the Omega of a life, of a world. From paucity to plenty, absence to abundance, we observe the "inner weather" (to borrow a term from Robert Frost) of the soul as it endures the constantly changing "outer weather" of the northern Midwestern landscape the poet inhabits. "The mercury stands at four above," the speaker states baldly in the volume's opening line, a Wisconsin Thoreau watching his pond. "Now winter earth, / beneath a cloudless sky / begins to feel a promise / of the sun," he concludes in the book's final words. The promise of that sun (a sure pun on "Son") constitutes the generative source of Block's poems and the hope that pervades them, no matter how dark they may sometimes seem.

And dark they are. "No lark ascends from sullen ground; / my prayers, a nest of broken shells," the speaker confides, invoking the Psalms, only his prayers founder instead of 'rising like incense.' "My prayers are chaff," "like empty bowls" that "rattle in the cupboard of my heart." This is how one keeps the "Prairie *Hours*"—faithful, watchful, attentive, even in a state of spiritual desolation.

Block's poems explore that desolation with tenderness and exactitude. All weather conditions have their attendant beauty, as do all spiritual states. In "Matins," a poem that seems simple on the page but plumbs depths of emotion in both speaker and attentive reader with its quietly insistent rhythm, repetition, and rhyme, the poet makes a plea:

Before the rising of the sun,
in deepest darkness,
be with me.
Before the pounding of my heart
in desperation, stay with me.

Such poems serve as prayers, incantations, talismans against grief and terror. Block provides a language of affliction, shedding light on the dark nights of the soul, enabling us to feel less alone, even when we may seem most abandoned.

Anno Domini also provides us with the antidote to our spiritual darkness, the consolations that relieve our desolations. A number of these poems take the form of Ignatian meditation wherein the speaker places himself beside Christ and narrates key moments of Jesus' ministry from the perspective of his disciples. Others channel the spirit of St. Francis of Assisi, who praises the beauty of the creation and celebrates a radically sacramental vision wherein the world bodies forth the God that made it. In "St. Francis and the Downy Woodpecker," the saint is full of gratitude as this splendid creature

takes my full attention—
making me forget
all the things that trouble me,
and helping me remember
Who made the downy be.

Block's poems gently acknowledge his masters, both the spiritual and the poetic. Echoes of Gerard Manley Hopkins, T.S. Eliot, Thomas Merton, and Denise Levertov haunt the volume—all poets who, like Block, regarded their art as sacramental practice. In his poem, "In the Forest of God's Mercy," the poet imagines Merton at work in his hermitage at Gethsemani Abbey in the hills of rural Kentucky:

His pen and brush become a prayer.
God lives in ferns
and tree rings, wagon wheels . . .
In the cottage, the icons glow,
half a world away,
in Asia, the archer bends his bow,
the string is taut.

This powerful scene evoked near the end of the volume provides an image not just of Merton but of every artist who pursues his or her craft with the fervor of faith. For both Merton and Block (as for Hopkins), 'the world is charged with the grandeur of God,' and the role of the poet is to make that Real Presence evident to others. There is an urgency to this work, as the image of the archer bending his bow on a distant continent suggests. Merton would die without warning and without having finished his life's labor, and for all the writer of *Anno Domini* knows, a similar fate awaits him. As Jesus once said, in sharp rebuke to those who faulted him for curing on the Sabbath, "*I must work the works of him that sent me while it is day: the night cometh, when no man can work.*"

*Anno Domini* is the fine fruit of one faithful poet's labor. The story that it tells is archetypal as well as personal—it is the poet's, surely, but it is also the reader's. We are all pilgrims, making our progress through the landscapes of desolation and consolation, through the seasons of doubt and despair, celebration and jubilation. Ed Block's poems bestow on the reader the blessing of making that pilgrimage in company rather than alone. Having wandered "Into Rough Country," as human beings are wont to do, together we travel

> to find a track,
> back uphill
> toward the light,
> avoiding crossroads
> of despair,
> seeking, instead,
> the sudden
> poetry of springs,
> some unexpected place of joy.

**Angela Alaimo O'Donnell**
Fordham University

ACKNOWLEDGMENTS

THE FOLLOWING POEMS FIRST appeared in the journals indicated.
"Midwinter Matins," in *Cross-Currents*

"Ordinary Time," "Confession to Sumac," "Sin," in *Review for Religious*

"John 8: 1-11," "After Christmas," "Transfiguration," "Christ has set us free," "Rue the Weeds," "New Joy," "Repentance," "Unclench my Spirit," in *Catechumenate*

"Candles at Easter," in *Emmanuel*

"The Saint as Imagined" (title "The Saint as Pictured") in *The Way of St. Francis*

"Dry Thoughts," in *Spiritus*

"Prairie *Hours*," in *Parabola*

Editorial assistance and artistic consultation by Sareene Proodian

# THE YEAR BEGINS

## Mid-Winter Matins

The mercury stands at four above.
The twigs I gather break and snap,
the falling sap froze dead within the wood.
The sun just up, the sky is bluish gray,
the promise of a brighter day.

This morning, in the dark, the dog beyond the road
barked once and fell to silence in the gloom.

The pines stood black against the morning sky,
the leafless trees like men and women
raising hands and arms in prayer.

And I remember Merton in his hermitage;
the overalls, the prayers, the everyday routines;
the sacramental fire, kindled,
bringing light and warmth to birth again.

## AFTER CHRISTMAS

The Christmas season's past.
The decorated tree still holds its air of grace.
The Wisemen at the crèche
remain for one last bow.

Ice crusts the heated bird bath;
sparrows perch upon the slippery rim
then dip their beaks and raise their heads.
Even at ten degrees they bathe.

The hopes of Advent hang among
the garlands and the bows.
The fact of Incarnation, like the later sun
these afternoons, or early morning light, has yet to dawn.

## ORDINARY TIME

Hoarfrost ages
the discarded Christmas trees.
Fog mutes the soul,
and dampness chills the heart.

In ordinary time
we wait, like puffed-out birds,
upon a frozen limb of time
and seek for solace in the hearing of the Word.

## CANDLES AT EASTER

Again the air is loud with birds,
the green of April mixed
with blue of sky and warmth of grass.
The evergreens are thrusting
delicate green candles
toward the sky.

The living spirit stirs the stems
and tendrils of our thoughts
and hearts. The candles
of our souls stand tall
with yearning for the Son.

## RUE THE WEEDS

Each spring, it seems,
a new weed
has its way
with us:

thorns, thistles,
creeping charlie,
quack grass,
and unheeded tares.

What makes us prone
to weeds that blight
our blooms and
ruin our fruit?
That choke
our very souls?

Good Husbandman,
be with us as we
tend our gardens,
rue the weeds.

## Spring Rain, Like Grace

Like grace,
the rain in finest mist
drifts down,
blessing the grass
and all around.

The robins hop on,
unaware. A pair of
nervous chipping sparrows—
a child's palm-width in size—
fly to the feeder,
perch on thinnest legs.

Each pecks a seed or two.
One bird looks puffed up.
Is it big with eggs? Or tufty
pulling feathers
from its breast to line the nest?

Like grace,
the rain in finest mist
drifts down,
blessing the grass
and all around.

## WHAT SPIRIT MOVES?

Evening, and a quiet
like the end of time
on earth. The June
birds fill the darkling
air with sound.
The night is cool.
What spirit visits us,
when day is done,
to claim us for its own?

## An Aunt's Legacy

A crucifix in needlepoint;
the yarn, like thread, in loops
of white and pink, and shading into purple,

appear like fragile snowflakes
touching at their sides, to form
the nave and transepts of a cross.

It hangs by a tassel
above my desk.
How many hours did she labor

on this gift, with fingers stiff
from age? With eyes grown cloudy,
legs gone numb?

Six tiny rose windows,
mandalas, ornate Catherine's wheels,
they speak her love, and care.

# PAIN AND PENITENCE

## Dry Thoughts

Dry thoughts in a dry time;

    the roots of things

        hang,

            poised to feel

                the spring.

No tendril penetrates

    the rocky soil.

        Dry wind combs out

            last autumn's hair.

In time of drought

        the dry ground yearns

            to feel the grace of flood.

## Prairie *Hours*

No lark at dawn
ascends from sullen ground;
my prayers, a nest
of broken shells.

By day my stubble fields
are whipped by winds of guilt;
my prayers are chaff.

At night my prayers,
like empty bowls,
rattle in the cupboard

of my heart,
as trains of sadness
rumble through the crossings
of my life.

# Sin

Sin dulls
the senses,
makes the heart
go lame in broken shoes.

Finding no peace,
the heart is sent,
a vagabond,
feet never coming home,
along the roughest paths,
amid the rocks temptations raise,
to hearth-warm sheets,
or peace, like honey in the comb.

## REPENTANCE

My spotless garment
now a twist of grimy rags,

I stumble to my knees
and claw the stony earth.

I cannot raise my eyes;
my neck is stiff
with sin and selfishness.

Renew me, Lord,
and wash me
in the river of your life.

# MATINS

Before the rising of the sun,
in deepest darkness,
be with me.

Before the pounding of my heart
in desperation,
stay with me.

## UNCLENCH MY SPIRIT, LORD

Tight clenched:
my heart and spirit,
like a fist.

Fingers grow numb,
the knuckles white
with selfishness and fear;

clenched tight around its
worries and its guilt,
my spirit scarcely feels.

Unclench my spirit, Lord,
but clasp me close to You.

## CONFESSION TO SUMAC

Sumac blooming,
innocent of motives,
sensuous seduction.

Red, orange, or scarlet;
blood, a Rothko,
Rauschenberg.

What it is, and must be,
one, with
no apologies.

The beauty of the trees
accuses me.
My greater gifts

I squander by my sins;
in dying autumn color
they proclaim

obedience unto death.
Rebellious, though, I
languish in the dark.

## Day By Day

Day by day,
        day by day;
                for thirty years,

                        you watched us,
        lived with us,
                broke bread,
                        broke wind,
washed feet
        drank wine
                with us.

You sat beside us
                arm to arm.
                        Your body smelled,
                        your breath was
rank, as bodies are.

You loved us,
                taught us,
                        heard our cries,
our lies, our stories.

You ate with us
                and spoke with us;

                then,
day by day,
        you died for us.

## THE SCAR

God has marked me,
I am His.
And how does that
now change my life?
At my age how am I to start
my life again?
New life,
like Nicodemus,
in the womb?

## THIS IS WHERE

This is where I need to be,
beneath Your cross
and on my knees.

Through sin forlorn
I stand alone.

A candle flickers
in my dark.

The air is cool
as is my heart.

Without Your grace
I'm doomed to be
no longer who I am,
no longer free.

## INTO ROUGH COUNTRY

I took a wrong way
late in life.
I veered
through thorn-thick
underbrush,
went wrong instead of right.

The path I chose
abandoned company,
ignored the watered valley,
led into rough country.

Now I try
to find a track,
back uphill
toward the light,
avoiding crossroads
of despair,
seeking, instead,
the sudden
poetry of springs,
some unexpected place of joy.

# GOOD NEWS MOMENTS

## CHRIST HAS SET US FREE
*Galatians 5:1*


It's hard to walk with Christ
at every step;
to lean upon the freedom of his love,
to feel the consolation:
sun on shoulders, wind in hair.

It's hard to walk with Christ;
to feel soft earth
beneath the grass,
the trees about me,
and to know that I am loved.

But walk I must,
and careful of the stone,
the thicket, thistle,
and the twisted path.

Yet dare I trust in Christ
with every breath;
as I step out
upon the trunk
that lies across the stream
and leads me over empty space,
and know that trunk,
and space,

and I
am Christ,
as well the torrent rushing on
below
is
Christ.

## John 8:1–11

You met the woman, threatened with death for adultery. You said, "Sin no more." What of us who are tempted every day?

Like an empty cistern,
well, or pond,
we're dry, and alkali.
This is a narrow, salty,
crusted time.
We crack and bleed
with fear, frustration,
sadness, guilt and pain.
Can we give anything while
lying in this state?
Not we, but You, through broken us.
Yet why must You be broken too?

## JOHN 21

'Out fishing with the boys all night,
and nothing caught.
A guy on shore says,
"How's the luck?"
"The fool," we think.
"Not good," we say.
"Then try the other side," he says.
"Is this guy nuts?" we think.
But, as a joke,
we toss the net.

Then, all at once,
it's full, and John
gets this idea;
"It's the Lord."

We're still a way
from shore.
How's John think he
can see that far?

But Pete jumps in,
then starts to wade.
We follow,
dragging net, and fish,

and all. On shore

there's fish and bread,
and how do we respond?
I dare not ask. I ought
to know.

## New Joy

And we've been told
to go and sin no more.
What joy to know
and feel

that our betrayal, our
faithlessness
is past—if not forgotten. Yes,
forgotten too.

We're sinners still,
but no!
He loves us into
joy,
and life
with him
again.

Jesus, your love
is greater than
our sinfulness;
your kindness
greater than
our fears.

## Walking On Water

"I need some time alone
to pray," he said.
Then he, and we
were gone;
we rowing toward
the north, against
a northeast wind
that scorned our efforts
all night long.

By three, we all
were tired, aching,
sweated from the work.

The sky above was dark,
but, to the east, the horizon—green
with dawn still hours off.

Yesterday he'd learned that
John was dead.
He fed the crowds—though
God knows how—
then left us.

Now, across the waves,
we saw him
walking on a point

of land, it seemed.
Yet we were fathoms
deep, the waves
rolled on, against us.

Peter called to him.
"Is it really you?"
Then, louder:
"If it's you, then
beckon me to
come."

The light was bad;
no one could see
his face, but first—
with head bowed down—

then looking up, he
opened his palms
and—even though
the winds were loud—
we heard a gentle
voice say, "come,
then."

Peter's triumphant laugh
was scarcely out when,
off his seat, he
jumped into the lake.

It bore him up. He
seemed surprised. No
shoal or bar, he

walked on water toward
the Lord. But when
our leader
looked up again—

a face of weariness and
grief—old Peter
had a pause. And then
a bigger wave came
crashing to his knees,

and he cried out,
"O, Rabbi, hold me up, or
I will surely drown."

The rest is told. And Jesus
pulled him up, admonished him,
the wind;
then joined us in the boat.
The wind subsided and
we made our way to shore.

## Up On The Mountain

Who's this guy we thought
we knew?
Suddenly he doesn't look
the same.
And it's like, there's
two other guys,
who look familiar, with him.

Talk about scared.
Who *is* this guy? Peter tries to break
the ice; suggests
three tents. It's something
to say.
And then it's dark; the clouds;
and then,
the voice.

## Transfiguration

Jesus,
You don't appear the same.
You frighten us.
We see your glory and,
like kids,
we are afraid.

Afraid of you,
ourselves, the world,
and choices that we've
made, or have to make.
Be with us,
in your glory, Lord!

# THREE FOR FRANCIS OF ASSISI

## FRANCIS AND THE DOWNY WOODPECKER

I'd like to hold
the downy in my hand,
whose squeak can make me smile;
whose cautious coming
to the suet feeder
through the branches
takes my full attention—
making me forget
all things that trouble me,
and helping me remember
Who made the downy be.

## Francis And The Lady Bugs Of Fall

The lady bugs
are swirling in
the warm October winds.
Like tiny, gentle
golden parachutes, they
ride the currents of the air.

May I be blown by
some far greater breeze,
whose Spirit cares
for all that lives.

## THE SAINT AS IMAGINED

A man at peace
so with himself,
that deer walk up to him,
and young birds—
only slowly—learn
their fear of humans,
even perching
on his tonsured head
and outstretched hand.

# IMAGINING THE KINGDOM

## O, Abundance!

O, to recognize abundance.

Pink and scalloped,
pearl-white, edged with pink,

magnolia blossoms at their ripest,
singular against an evening sky,

set off by dark boughs, tiny branches,
tracery behind the plethora

of petals, shading pastel pink
as sunset falls.

They almost speak
their delicacy;

hang pensive, pendant
in the cooling evening air.

Regal bouquet,
lifted aloft to cloudless sky

like opened palms,
each blossom fronts the cloudless sky.

But rain, tomorrow, will spell
the end of all this radiant abundance,

this natural glory of a single week
in spring.

## I HAVE CALLED YOU EACH BY NAME (ISAIAH 43:1)
### *(for Beckah)*

A spark will light the eyes
and suddenly a clerk
becomes a person anyone can love.
Look at the name tag.
Call her Beckah, call him Tran.

In shops and motels, pharmacies,
the cleaner's, deli, fast food chain:
address the workers by the names they wear,
remark the change.
                              Across a gulf of cold
impersonality, formality, and anonymity,
reach out a glance, extend
a smile. With little risk we lighten
burdens, make the day move
more swiftly for other human beings,
their personhood, called forth,
a fullness, ripe with possibilities.

## Sparrow In Fall

A chipping sparrow
crouches in the sun
beneath
a Black Hills fir.

The air is chill,
the sky is blue.
What further need of
proof
that our Creator lives?

## AT VESPERS

From burning bush
to tongues of flame,
from incense rising
to descending dove,
You make Your
presence known to us.

## In The Forest Of God's Mercy
*(Thomas Merton 1915-1968)*


In a cottage of concrete block
beyond the mountain
among Kentucky hardwoods,
a monk—escaped at last—
a balding man in scapular and work boots,
builds a fire, sweeps the floor
with broom and hardened hands.

He prays his *Pater* and his *Ave*,
drinks strong tea and reads
a book by oil lamp,
writes at a plain wood table.

Alone in the woods in every weather,
loving what is most frail,
his eye and soul a lens
that sees into the essence of it all.

Even his pen and brush become a prayer.
He sees God in the ferns
and tree rings, wagon wheels
and rocks, abandoned barns.

He sits in darkness, seeking
a deeper silence, the savage
innocence of nature, his life

now hidden with Christ, in God.
Alone, yet wedded to a world
confused, bewildered, searching,
he strives toward wholeness,
Being both within and all around.

In the cottage, the icons glow,
while half a world away,
in Asia, the archer bends his bow,
the string is taut.

# A Death In Autumn

Frost tonight;
the bluffs are orange,
the sumac, turning red.
And now a mother, friend,
has gone to God.

The Minnesota autumn comes again
and warns of winter's cold.

A hundred autumns—more—and now
with drums we lay you down.
With drums we say farewell.

Your husband, decades gone
before you, welcomes you,
and all the saints.

Decades in a home
of native stone
beneath a Minnesota bluff,
you lived a life of quiet faith,
a life of taste that valued
family and friends.

A hundred, hundred autumns—
and more springs—
we wish you, now, in your eternal home.

## Hope Grows Slowly

Hope grows slowly on autumn boughs
blown clean of leaves; in pear tree buds,
gray, pointed buds of magnolia,
and the limbs of sumac, fuzzy as the white
tail's antlers at the start of fall.

Deep in their roots, persistent life
rises slowly into the stems,
preparing patiently for spring,
long months of cold and snow away.

## AT CHRISTMAS

The holydays are here.
The graces fall like snowflakes all around.
The gifts beneath the tree
and friends are gathered.
At every moment
Jesus touches us with gentleness.

## The Christmas Cards

The Christmas cards we put away
will spell the season's end,
and a measure of the joy
they brought with them.

Old friends and relatives,
forgotten for a year,
return in photographs of children,
pets, and families,
then, jumbled in a drawer,
or pressed between the pages
of an address book,
become occasions for reflection,
gratitude, and prayer.

## January Thaw

A crust of sleet melts
from the south sides
of the furrows
in the garden,
leaving stripes of white,
creating fractal patterns
at the margins of the ice.

The locust at the garden's edge
wears hoarfrost on its limbs,
and pale green lichen on its
northern sides. Its aged bark
burns black and gray against
the melting snow.

The winter earth,
beneath a cloudless sky,
begins to feel a promise
of the sun.

www.ingramcontent.com/pod-product-compliance
Lightning Source LLC
LaVergne TN
LVHW051709080426
835511LV00017B/2820